# #MAXOUT
# YOUR LIFE

## STRATEGIES FOR
## BECOMING AN ELITE
## PERFORMER

## ED MYLETT

ISBN: 978-1-64184-029-3

Mylett Communications

# CONTENTS

# PREFACE

There are 86,400 seconds in a day. We each have the same 1,440 minutes to spend however we choose. Each of these minutes are precious moments. Some moments will be memorable, some regretful, and too many of them will be wasted.

Time is measured by our birth and death. How we use those moments in between determine the quality of our lives. Hour by hour, minute by minute, these small units of time are too often filled with little things that really seem to matter at the time. Seeking small pleasures, avoiding minor discomforts, and pursuing trivial goals. We are too easily offended, and too consumed with the opinions of others. If we're not careful, we simply begin to exist and not really live.

The average lifespan for a person is seventy-eight years. Of those years, twenty-eight will be spent sleeping, and seven of those sleeping years are spent lying awake at night with worry.

Factor in the average eleven years watching television or surfing the internet, ten and a half years working, four years driving, the years spent eating, getting dressed, and doing mundane tasks, and it leaves approximately *eight years to live your life*. If you were told right now that you had only eight years left in this life, what would that do to your sense of urgency? How deep would your gratitude for each moment become?

The challenge is we don't know how many of these moments we actually get. If you've ever spoken to someone at the end of their life, you will often hear expressions of regret, missed chances, and opportunities. They recount how quickly life passed and not to take it for granted. I am often asked how I've made the most out of my moments as I strive to #MaxOut my life. That is exactly why I've written this book. I want to help as many people as possible by sharing some of the techniques that have served me throughout my life.

Each moment is fleeting and precious and we know it. Why then do most people choose to let those moments slip away? I'm fascinated with maxing out every area of my life while I am here. I want to explore what is attainable. It all comes down to having experiences that create memories and legacy after we're gone. There is so much value in pushing past an existence of just getting by and designing a life that you can #MaxOut.

I believe we are all born with blessings, gifts, and purpose. I think the recipe for a happy life is to discover your unique blessings and gifts, be driven by your purpose, and to use those to fulfill your destiny. The journey of discovering your gifts or blessings, and how to use them as you chase down your purpose, *is* your life's story. How will the script of your life read? What story will be told? Will you discover a little of your purpose and go a few miles down the road? Will you push to uncover more and go a little farther? Or will you fight to reveal all your gifts and blessings and go as far as you possibly can? Will you #MaxOut this life?

My hope for this book is that the details of my experiences, strategies, and guidance help you to achieve your next level of living. I want to help you uncover your purpose and embrace your blessings, so you pursue the best version of your life. What if you could see what that looks like? What if there is a version of you that achieved your maximum potential? What if, when you reach the end of this life, you could meet the ultimate version of who you were capable of becoming? The question is: would the man or woman you had become resemble that version, or would you be total strangers?

I believe we all have a destiny version of ourselves, the person we were born to be.

The version of us that took risks. The version that walked the road less traveled, overcame adversities and achieved our true potential. I think of it like we all have a twin. This version of us who's lived the life we are born to live and reached our full potential. That person is waiting for us on the other side after we pass. When my time here is finished, and I meet my maker, it is my hope that the Lord tells me, "Well done, good and faithful servant." I also envision a sort of ceremonial exit where I am introduced to the man I was born to be, that I was supposed to be and destined to be. I want to shake hands with that man, and I want to be his identical twin. I don't want there to be a huge gap between my reality and the man I had the potential to be. Instead I want them to be perfectly matched; that's my mission. Every decision I make, every action I take, is measured against one simple question: *Will this get me closer to the man I was born to be?*

That is how you #MaxOut! I hope to teach and share with you some of the methods I've used to improve the key areas of my life. I believe this book gives you definitive steps towards achieving the ultimate and best version of you. The YOU that you were born to be.

# 1

# EDDIE SPAGHETTI

*Things Happen FOR Me, Not TO Me*

Someone recently interviewed me at my home. After looking around at all the material blessings—the big house, fast cars, and nice things—they asked me what I appreciate most about my home on a daily basis. The obvious answer, the one that's pretty hard to miss, is the fact that my backyard is the ocean! That's a pretty great thing, but honestly, a close second is pulling the shower faucet on every morning and having the water hit me in the face.

When I first started building my business, things were really tough. Our house was foreclosed

11

on, my wife's car was repossessed, and the power was shut off. All of those things are difficult, but the worst was when the water was shut off. If you've ever been through this, then you know what I mean. You can't cook. You can't shower. You can't wash the dishes or brush your teeth. It's the absolute worst place to be in.

At the time, I was newly married to my wife. Every morning, we'd get up early and gather our clothes before anyone else in our apartment complex was up. We'd walk down the stairs in the cold and use the outdoor shower at the complex's pool. I would hold up a towel to give my wife privacy because the shower didn't have a door. I remember feeling so ashamed walking back upstairs to our apartment, hoping no one had seen us.

I was that broke. I had to leave the pool shower, put on a suit, and pretend I was a successful entrepreneur as I built my business. I fought a mental and emotional battle of chasing my dream while I struggled through the nightmare of my reality.

Entrepreneurship is riddled with false starts. You'll take a couple of steps forward, get a little success, and then you'll face an obstacle that pulls you back. However, it's not all bad. You will never be back to square one because each experience is progress if you've learned a lesson. If you genuinely understand how to achieve real success, you recognize that obstacles and setbacks are necessary. They strengthen and test you. They prepare you for anything and everything life will continue to throw at you. When you are experiencing the setback, take it as an encouraging sign and keep pushing through.

I can relate to the struggles that all entrepreneurs go through when they are building their business because I almost quit *several times.* In the beginning, I had my share of adversity and disappointments. Being an entrepreneur is the most tremendous personal development program in the history of the world, with a massive compensation package attached. It is also one of the greatest self-awareness and self-discovery processes you will ever go through.

The first thing you should know about me, is I am a normal dude. I didn't start out with millions in the bank. I know what it's like to fall on hard times and start from the bottom. As a young man, I was insecure and shy. Confidence does not come naturally to me, and I lacked it for most of my youth.

As a kid, I was smaller than most boys my age and got teased a lot for it. I was a target and bullied until about the 5th grade. I was so little and thin, kids would call me "Eddie Spaghetti." Somewhere along the line, someone was kind enough to complement that label with, "your meatballs are ready," making it quite a melody when recited. This certainly impacted my identity, making me reclusive, insecure, and self-conscious. When you combine that with my shy and introverted nature, it was a recipe for low self-esteem.

As I grew up, I developed a passion for baseball. For many children, sports tend to reveal certain physical gifts and shine a light on them. It gives kids a place to belong and show a capacity that they may not have seen inside themselves before. My gift was speed and strong hand-eye coordination. I became a solid hitter. My skills strengthened as I grew, and throughout high school, it was clear I was good enough to take it further. This part of my childhood was a turning point in my confidence. Being good at something improves confidence. I developed my skills even more and began to see myself as a winner. I put in the work, so I expected to win.

I continued to play in college but experienced an injury that would end my baseball career permanently. I was hit with a pitch in the right calf during a game and did not realize the extent of the damage. When I went in for examination, it was determined that a non-cancerous tumor had formed and had to be removed. The procedure removed the tumor and a portion of my calf that immobilized me for eight months. After the cast was removed, the doctors found that a second tumor had formed. It was also non-cancerous. After many consultations, I decided to leave the benign tumor in my leg, and it is still there to this day.

This too was a turning point in my youth. Baseball had been the way I earned recognition and accomplishment. It was where I had earned respect from my peers.

I was not prepared for a Plan B. I had no backup plan and had to discover what other paths I should take. I was devastated and without direction. We don't always understand why something is happening when it occurs. It's usually only in hindsight that its purpose is revealed.

Looking back, I know that my childhood dream coming to an end was the beginning of my life's true purpose and destiny.

After my surgery, I found myself living back at home with my mom and dad, sleeping in my old bed, surrounded by stuff from my childhood. I was broke, unemployed, and spent my days watching TV shows like Maury Povich and Jerry Springer. It was pretty pathetic. With my baseball career over, who was I? I knew I couldn't go back to being Eddie Spaghetti, but I struggled with identity and what my future held for me.

One day, my dad came home and said, "Hey, I found you a job! Tomorrow morning you've gotta get up and go to McKinley Home for Boys."

McKinley is a campus of group-homes for boys who were removed from their homes for reasons ranging from abuse to being orphaned. I was a young, twenty-one-year-old kid and suddenly I was thrown into a totally new environment. I was living and working with these young boys day in and day out. It was amazing. After the horrible situations these boys had been through, they just wanted to be loved and for someone to believe in them. I became like a big brother to them, and it transformed my life. Helping them build their self-confidence and learn to believe in a better life began to shape my new identity.

Suddenly, it wasn't all about me anymore. It wasn't about my ego and wanting to be rich and famous. It was about how I could help them. Give value to them. Improve their lives. I wanted to help these young boys rewrite their stories. I wanted to help them realize their dreams and discover their power. These boys came from a life of trying to survive, and I was trying to get them to change from a mindset of survival mode to #MaxOut their lives.

That's when I realized becoming a professional baseball player was never my true destiny. That's what everyone told me and expected of me. It was my "story." However, my baseball career coming to an end actually happened *for* me, not *to* me. It allowed me to find my real passion, which is helping people discover their God-given gifts and teach them to live life with purpose.

It was during this time that I was introduced to my current business. At first, it was a means to make additional income working part-time. It allowed me to continue working with the boys until my business began to take off. In this new venture, I was able to also help people and feel good about my work. It was rewarding both emotionally and financially. I approached my new business from a place of genuinely wanting to better people's lives. Because I enjoyed it, my passion further fueled my work ethic and laid a strong foundation for success.

As I built my financial services business, I started to notice that many adults are living similarly to the way those boys lived in the group homes. Living in *survival mode*. I don't believe people were born into a life merely to survive it. I believe each of us is here with a purpose. While many people give up on discovering their purpose, I assume that because you're reading this, you intend to find yours. You are here to #MaxOut.

My motto was, and still is: *People matter, things don't.*

I spent the first part of my life building a legacy. I became a seven-figure earner by age thirty, and an eight-figure earner by age forty with a nine-figure net worth. That success has allowed me to shift much of my daily focus to helping others realize their full potential to #MaxOut their lives.

About a year ago, I made a decision to publicly share the knowledge I've gained through years of building my career, being a peak performance expert, and coaching some of the top athletes and entrepreneurs in the world. Prior to that, I'd lived an intentionally private life. I'm naturally an introverted person, and fairly quiet, so this was a big transition for me.

At the prompting of many close friends and clients, I stepped out of my comfort zone and started the #MaxOut movement. I created it to provide strategies and inspiration to help people around the world reach their maximum potential.

For me, the idea of #MaxOut came when my son Max was six years old. One day, I took him with me to the local car wash. As we sat waiting, a gentleman struck up a conversation with me about how children are always growing and changing. He looked at Max, then said to me, "Enjoy this age. Enjoy the six-year-old version of him because when he's seven, the six-year-old is gone forever!" When he said that, I immediately wondered when he stopped growing and changing, and why most people stop growing and changing.

Without really thinking it through, I replied, "When did that stop for you, sir? Growing?" It occurred to me that letting go of the old version of one's self is not something to mourn but rather to celebrate. We should always be in the process of changing and becoming the next, best version of ourselves.

Benjamin Franklin said, "Most men die at age twenty-five, but we just don't get around to burying them until they are seventy-five." That is referring to the fact that most people never live a fulfilling life. They stop doing what the six-year-old version of them used to do. They stop growing and progressing and simply exist, spending years and even decades as the same version of themselves. For some, once they reach a milestone birthday, they have a "mid-life" crisis. Not for me. I want to be constantly growing, constantly striving to reach the ultimate version of me. Regardless of my age, I'm never going to stop chasing down the man I was born to be.

I'm on a quest—a life mission—to never be the same version of me, year after year. For me, it is a crisis. I am constantly evolving and adapting my thinking, my methods of communication, fitness, and all areas of my life. Recently, my teenage daughter jokingly asked me if I was in a mid-life crisis. She was teasing me a bit about my level of social media posting and my recent change in appearance with a beard. I thought about her question and responded "Yes!" I am in a mid-life crisis. In fact, I am in a *daily* life crisis and I aim to be in a *lifelong* crisis as I continue to grow. When I was twenty-five, I was in a crisis to not be the same version of me when I was twenty-six. Same when I was thirty-four, same when I was forty-five, and I hope I will still be in the same crisis when I'm seventy-five.

Maybe this seems over the top. For the average person, it absolutely is. Not everyone is interested in achieving their maximum potential. This book is for the crazies. The ones that wake up in the morning wanting to be better than they were yesterday. The ones that can't turn it off, even if they tried. The ones that will not accept less than giving it their all. The ones that want to #MaxOut.

# 2

# #MAXOUT YOUR DAY

*Habits and Rituals of Elite Performers*

We are what we do. It's as simple as that. Having a consistent and specific routine has been crucial in helping me achieve the level of success, contribution, and peace of mind I have today.

Most people think they need to be motivated to get up and go to work every day and continuously seek motivation. The real separator between successful and average people is that successful people do it whether they are motivated or not! Don't misunderstand me. Inspiration and motivation are prerequisites in maxing out any circumstance, but they are never your constant companions.

Habits and rituals are what carry us through on the days when we aren't motivated. People have the misconception that it's the most motivated people who are the ones winning, but that's not the case. Extraordinary habits are what allow people to perform at an elite level, even on the days they are not motivated. For more details on how to #MaxOut, listen to my podcast on iTunes or go to edmylett.com/podcasts and listen to "The Keys to #MaxingOut."

If you're not motivated, get to work! Let your motivation come from doing the work. This is the catalyst for motivation, not the other way around. The process of taking action can generate motivation.

I rely heavily on my rituals and routines when "discipline" fails. When you're weak, tired, and under pressure, your mind and body go into habit mode. That is why it's so important to create habits that serve you—they keep you on track, even on days when you aren't "feelin' it." That's what separates elite performers from everyone else.

What I've found is, if I can control the beginning and end of my day, then I'm much more likely to control the middle. Most people lose control of their day in the first ten minutes because they wake up worried and stressed without positive habits, and they begin to *react* to it immediately. If you don't have structure to help keep control of your day (proactive), then you are susceptible to whatever life throws at you (reactive). Being reactive prevents you from making strategic decisions, and you just go where life kicks you. Developing habits that provide structure give you a greater chance of operating proactively versus reactively.

I am often asked what my morning and daily routines consist of, so I wanted to share my personal morning habits so you can implement into your life what works for you. This routine has worked for me for many years and enables me to stay focused, fit, and mentally ready for each day.

## MY MORNING ROUTINE:

### 1. Get up early.

Getting a lot of sleep is overrated. It's the quality of your sleep that matters, not the quantity. My evening routine prepares me for deep sleep so that I'm able to make the most of my sleep. Elite performers operate on less sleep than "normal" people. I'm obviously not a doctor, but for me, six hours is more than adequate to get quality, restorative sleep.

Success demands that you rise before the sun. A primary trait in elite performers is their commitment to attacking their day early—to #MaxOut each day. Rise before the sun every day!

I get about six hours of sleep a night. Why? Because nothing productive is happening when I'm sleeping! I'm not calling people, I'm not influencing people, I'm not changing the world or making money. *I'm sleeping.*

I truly believe that the amount of rest you need to win is minimal. I start my day between 4:30 and 5:00 a.m. every day (except Sunday).

Sunday's are my make-up day. It's the one day each week where I get as close to eight hours as I can. Monday through Saturday, I'm up and done with my daily routine before most people get out of bed. I will add that sleep experts say you can't make-up lost sleep, so this might not work for you, but it's what has worked for me for many years.

One reason why oversleeping is so counter-productive is that it immediately starts your day off stressed and disorganized, causing you to play catch up all day long (reactive).

Champions are proactive.

**Here's an easy way to reduce your time spent sleeping** that will not burn you out. Reduce your sleep by fifteen minutes a week. Don't make a drastic change and go from getting up at 8:00 a.m. to waking up at 5:00 a.m. That won't work. You'll be exhausted by 3:00 p.m. and quit after a few days. It's much better to ease yourself into it by getting up fifteen minutes earlier for a week at a time. After you have a week under your belt and your body has begun adjusting to the new time, cut your sleep by another fifteen minutes the next week.

Even reducing your sleep by one hour will make a major impact on your life and your business. One extra hour a day is 365 additional hours each year for you to WIN! Over a five-year period, that's the equivalent of adding seventy-six productive work days to your business, or towards achieving your goals. It's a way to literally *get more time* in your day. For more details on my morning and night routines go to edmylett.com/podcasts and listen to "Ed's Morning Routine," as it covers my routines with more specificity.

## 2. Hydrate.

The first thing I do when I get out of bed in the morning is drink a liter of water. I set it on my nightstand when I go to bed so that it's right there waiting for me when my feet hit the floor. It's the first thing I do; I hydrate myself for the day. This is not something to overlook. Dehydration thickens your blood and can negatively impact your blood pressure, cholesterol, make your organs work harder, cause headaches, etc. This robs you of energy and will prevent you from performing at your very best.

### 3. Cold morning, warm night.

Every morning I do something cold, right off the bat. Cold stimulates our fight or flight response in our body and completely awakes our cellular nervous system. This gets us fully awake quickly, keeping us from feeling groggy or tired.

To get this benefit, you could splash cold water on your face, take a cold shower, or even walk or stand outside in the cold for a few minutes.

I live oceanfront and lakefront, so I jump in the cold ocean or the lake. If I can't do that, I take a cold shower. It doesn't have to be for long. I keep the shower cold for about a minute, and it instantly rejuvenates me and gives me the energy to start my day.

Be sure to warm up afterward; we don't want anyone getting sick or catching a cold. The idea here is to shock your system into a fully awake-state, and once you're there, get warm! I realize this seems a bit extreme and may not be for everyone, but it works very well for me.

## 4. Do quick breathing and stretching exercises.

I do them very quickly. You can find some easy instructional stretching and breathing videos online; be sure to choose ones that work for you. Commit to spending a few minutes each morning warming up your body and providing a burst of oxygen to your brain.

## 5. A few minutes of quiet.

I take a few minutes each day to pray in the morning. It helps me feel connected, peaceful, and balanced. I practice meditation as well. It's one of my favorite ways to center and focus myself. You can practice whatever faith, gratitude, or mindfulness techniques that help get you mentally centered and focused on the day ahead.

## 6. Get your thoughts set for the day.

Whatever your mind is thinking about first thing in the morning is what it will be looking for throughout the day. I learned a technique from Tony Robbins over twenty years ago, and I still do it *every single morning.* To help me control what I focus on and remain in charge of my thoughts, I ask myself these questions.

- What am I **happy** about in my life right now? What about it makes me happy, and how does it make me feel?

- What am I **excited** about in my life right now? What about it makes me excited, and how does that make me feel?

- What am I **proud** of in my life right now? What about it makes me proud, and how does that make me feel?

- What am I **grateful** for in my life right now? What about it makes me grateful, and how does that make me feel?

- What am I **enjoying** most in my life right now? What about it am I enjoying, and how does that make me feel?

- What am I **committed** to in my life right now? What about it makes me committed, and how does that make me feel?

- Who do I **love**? Who loves me? How does that make me feel?

Most people roll out of bed in the morning and start worrying. *What do I have to do today? What bills do I have to pay?* They are starting the day in a negative mindset for the first twenty seconds they're awake!

What if you rolled out of bed with your mind programmed to think thoughts that will *serve you?* What if you started each day asking yourself, *What are you happy and excited about; what are you proud of?* Can you see how empowered you would feel? You'd be ready to take on whatever life has in store for you each day.

I used to be the kind of guy who woke up stressed and tired. Making these questions part of my morning routine has made a powerful, long-term difference in my thinking and beliefs.

Once you've made this a habit, your mind will go to work throughout the day to find the answers to these questions and drawing these experiences into your life. It will find more of what you're proud of, what you love, what you give, what you're grateful for, and what you learn. When this becomes your ritual, your mind begins to find the answers to the questions it knows you will ask yourself at the end of the day.

Remember, the quality of your life is equal to the quality of questions you ask yourself.

## 7. WORK OUT.

The next thing I do every single morning is work out. Do some type of physical activity to start your day. It could be stretching, walking, yoga, biking, running, or whatever you do to stay active. It needs to be something!

Personally, I go to the gym five days a week and spend sixty to ninety minutes doing something physical. I believe that a successful businessperson is a business *athlete*. They treat themselves great, they train and prepare, and being physically active is a big part of that.

Don't make the mistake of overcommitting yourself to start. You want fitness to be a lifelong habit you keep, not something that you'll easily burn yourself out on. Fitness and nutrition are the biggest areas people struggle to keep their promises to themselves. Every year, the gym is most crowded in the month of January, and then by February many of the newly committed have quit. The common mistake people make is to do too much too soon. Set challenging goals you know you'll be able to accomplish, and then you can increase them as you progress. For more details on my workout routine go to edmylett.com/podcasts and listen to "Ed's Fitness Regimen."

## 8. Eat.

I nourish my body. I know many of you might skip breakfast, but please don't. It's such an important part of a healthy lifestyle. A healthy breakfast provides the much-needed energy and strength to #MaxOut your day.

While I eat, I catch up on the news, check my email, and listen to inspirational content, but *never* before breakfast. Before I allow anything in, I want my mind to be clear of distraction. I want to remain as unaffected by what's going on in the outside world for as long as I can each morning. This time is sacred. It's dedicated to helping me get focused and start my day in a positive direction (proactive).

Depending on my workout, steps 7 and 8 are reversed.

**Actions are rituals;** they are the repeatable things we do every single day. They have a huge impact on our lives whether we know it or not. What we do consistently over and over is what produces results, or on the flip side, what prevents us from getting the results we seek. When rituals and habits are intentional and positive, we naturally shift into autopilot, propelling us towards our goals. They are *that* powerful.

Duke University did a study which showed that 40% of the actions people take each day do not require a decision because they are simply habitual actions. Forty percent of our daily actions! That's *huge*.

This ritual thing is mind-blowing!

We are truly creatures of habit. Think about it. Most of us get up in the morning and do the same sequence of actions every day. We put the coffee on, brush our teeth, and take a shower. We do the exact same things, in the same order, without ever needing to stop and think about it.

Habits happen on cue. That cue signals you to move into non-thinking, or "habit mode." This can be great if your habits are serving you, but it can also be the cause of what's sabotaging you.

Therefore, it stands to reason that the person with the best rituals and habits *wins*.

**What are your habits?** What habits have you formed around work? Do you go into the office before everyone else and get right to work? Or are you always running late and spend the first thirty minutes catching up with your colleagues? What are the cues that get you to take action? What new cues could you put in place to help create new, positive habits?

The power is in your hands. Take control of your habits.

Our capacity to change, once we focus all our energy on the area we want to improve, is *massive*. Focus on it completely. Get obsessed. Obsess over your goals. Obsess over changing your beliefs and thoughts. People underestimate their capacity to become laser-focused on one area and master it.

## NIGHT ROUTINES:

**Warm night.** Before bed, I try to take a warm sauna, bath, or shower before bed to relax my body and help my nervous system prepare for sleep. I do, however, keep the bedroom cool. For optimal sleep, specialists recommend a room temperature between 60 and 67 degrees Fahrenheit.

I cut out caffeine and limit food intake five hours before I intend to sleep. Cutting out the caffeine is obvious, but the case can be argued either way for food intake prior to bed. For me, I am focused on my fitness and don't believe in adding extra calories before going into a state of rest. The other reason is that digestion requires your body to expend energy when it should be resting. The key is to get better quality sleep over quantity.

Additionally, I cut out any blue-screen exposure (computer, phone, or television) at least thirty minutes before bed. Multiple studies have shown blue-light to impact our sleep patterns and our natural clocks. Instead, I spend the last thirty minutes to an hour preparing for the next day.

I layout my clothes, go over my appointments, and review my goals. Reviewing goals prior to sleep ensures my mind focuses on those and goes to work on them while I rest.

I also like to do some light stretching before bed and take some quiet time to reflect on my daily gratitude, prayer, and to ask myself these questions:

1. What have I given today? In what ways have I been a giver today?

2. What did I learn today?

3. How has today added to the quality of my life? How can I use today as an investment in my future?

What are you grateful for? Whenever you're going through something tough, stop and think: *What am I grateful for in this moment?* Whether it's your family, or your home, or being alive, gratitude is the antidote to most of our pain.

You can't be grateful and be a victim at the same time. Stop playing the blame game. Success is inside; it comes from *you*. It's not reacting to the outside world or other people; it is only created by you and your higher power. Play the game of happiness, faith, and abundance.

These rituals help me to obtain a deeper level of sleep.

**There are only two things that matter when it comes to success:**

1. The reasons why you are doing it.

2. And the results.

There are no excuses. Stop making excuses for failing because once you do that, you are tolerating failure. You are allowing it to exist.

Remember, we are all naturally programmed to have routines and habits. We just might not be conscious of them. You already have a daily process you follow without so much as a second thought. Whether it's waking up and checking your phone or getting into the shower and soaping your body, shampooing your hair, and then grabbing your toothbrush. Whatever your routine is, you do it subconsciously the same way every day.

Be cognizant of those habits because they are a preview of your future. Unlike inspiration or motivation, those are your constant companions, and it is critical that you master them so they don't master you. I'm not unique in having a routine like this. I've simply chosen to follow one that will help me reach my goals and live my best life.

I urge you to take an inventory of what your current habits and rituals are—ones you might not have previously been aware of—and begin taking steps immediately to control them.

# 3

# #MAXOUT YOUR MIND

## *Change Your Thoughts to*
## *Change Your Beliefs*

What are your core beliefs? What do you believe to be true about yourself? About your God? About your future? What do you believe about your potential?

And the big question: **What do you believe you are *worth*?**

What you believe about yourself governs everything in your life. Beliefs become a self-fulfilling prophecy. We must be extremely aware of them and guard them at all costs.

Our thoughts create our beliefs, and one way to change your thinking is to change the quality of the questions you ask yourself.

The average person has 75,000 thoughts every day, and 91% are *exactly* the same as the day before. It isn't hard to see why so many people stay in the exact spot in life as it relates to relationships, career, finance, fitness, etc. (Read this slowly.) Do you ever *think about* what you think about? Thoughts are like magnets; they draw to you that which you think about regularly. They also create the filter you see the world through. If you want real change, you must first change what you are thinking about. Change just 10% of your thoughts, and you can dramatically change your life! That is powerful, and it is under *your control*. Changing your environment and associations is key to changing your thoughts because it breaks your routine and comfort level. Your identity must be raised and challenged (more on this in Chapter 4).

**Your subconscious thoughts are always trying to prove you right.** We've all heard the saying that you are what you think about. Here is some insight as to why your mind is so powerful.

**You have a mental filter that can work with you, or against you.**

*Pay close attention to this topic because it is the most important part of my success.* There is a bundle of nerves at our brainstem called the Reticular Activating System (RAS) that acts as a gatekeeper, filtering out irrelevant information and allowing only relevant information to enter our awareness. This little bit of brain matter is responsible for filtering out the massive amounts of information that your body, and the world around it, is constantly throwing its way. It filters out all the things that would prove our beliefs false, and instead works overtime on filtering *in* all the things that will prove our beliefs true.

Your RAS takes what you focus on and creates a filter for it. It then sifts through the data and presents only the pieces that are important to you. All of this happens without you noticing, of course. The RAS programs itself to work in your favor without you actively doing anything.

That is powerful, isn't it?

When you believe you're going to grow a big successful business or have a great income, the RAS starts working to filter in all the experiences that will prove this to be your reality. Specifically, if you believe people need what you have, the RAS will begin to reveal opportunities that may have always been there but are now highlighted as a result of your focus. This focus causes them to be relevant to you. Conversely, it will begin filtering out everything that would prove you to be unsuccessful.

Have you ever bought a new car, and all of a sudden, you see that exact car everywhere? Why have you never noticed it before? And why are they suddenly *everywhere* you look? You thought your blue Honda was unique, but now all you see are blue Hondas. Your RAS will even see them on the other side of the freeway! They've been there all along, but now the RAS is filtering them into your awareness, causing you to notice them whereas before they were unimportant to you and irrelevant.

If you're focused on growing your business by constantly looking for new prospects, you'll suddenly hear a conversation three tables away at a restaurant that will instantly grab your attention. Why? Because the topic of that conversation somehow relates to your business and you instantly recognize how your services could help that individual, turning them into a prospect. Had you not been hyper-focused on recognizing potential client needs, you would never have heard that conversation. You hear it now because it matters to you, and the RAS has filtered it in. That's your "blue Honda."

The sad thing is that most people don't know how to control the RAS in a positive way. Their "blue Hondas" are their problems—all the things going wrong in their life. So, what shows up for them? More problems, more things going wrong in their life. Escape this cycle at all costs by obsessing about what you want and not what you *don't* want.

The RAS only takes in what you have deemed most important by your habitual mental setup.

Anything you want in your life requires your total obsession. Remember this: *Your obsessions become your possessions.* That's how the RAS begins working in your favor.

Understand that the RAS does not attract the things you need. Everything you need has always been there. You just didn't see them because they were not deemed significant at the time. Once you focus on a goal, your obsession and RAS are heightened, and you filter in all the elements that support your goal. You literally begin to see, hear, and feel things that always existed, but never noticed before. The RAS is the greatest tool and magnet for success in the world. It is a God-given survival tool that we all possess but rarely utilize.

Another example is your own name. If you are in a loud crowd of people and someone yells your name (even if it isn't intended for you), you hear it because your RAS has had a lifetime of focus on it. So, the key to making your RAS work for you is to make the things you want as important to you as your own name.

If your belief is, "I'm going to attract great people into my life," your RAS will start shedding all the people in your life who no longer align with this belief, and it starts filtering in the people who do.

My mother-in-law is a great example of this. She's an amazing woman of faith, and she's always looking for signs of God showing up in her life. Every time we're together, she points out the evidence. She'll see a guy at the grocery store showing kindness to an elderly woman, and she'll say, "Isn't God wonderful?" She notices good things everywhere! She's going to notice anything good that happens because she's looking for it. The law of the subconscious mind delivers to her what she believes to be true.

It's the simplest things that she notices and recognizes as God's presence in her life. She'll walk outside, and when the wind blows and hits her face she will say, "Thank you, Jesus." She sees

God in *everything* all day long, and she's the happiest person I know.

Her life is abundant because she's always looking for and noticing her blessings. She's trained her RAS to search for goodness, and that's what is constantly showing up in her life. Many times, those are the very same things that are around you and I, but we don't notice them because our RAS has not been trained to support that same belief, therefore it filters them out.

**Viruses in your mind** Your life becomes what your thoughts and beliefs have been. Are you going to be a *scarcity* thinker? Always focusing on what you *don't* have? Or are you going to be an abundance thinker? Always grateful for what you *do* have?

Life is not about *overcoming* and *struggling*—that is a flawed mindset. If you think you are constantly struggling or battling through adversity and difficulty, your mind will constantly attract struggles and battles to you. As difficult as it is to accept, you've allowed those struggles into your life because your mindset is flawed. Instead, maintain the mindset of "things are happening *for me*. My life is winning. It's filled with peace, happiness, and success."

Flawed thinking is a virus of your mind. Once there is a virus in a computer, it slows down and becomes sluggish. In a worst-case scenario, it crashes. This is what happens when people get a virus in their mind. They are slowed down in their pursuit of goals. Their mind is sidetracked with noise and clutter. This makes achieving goals nearly impossible, and the mind will shift into survival mode.

**You only get from life what you will tolerate**. If the most important areas of your life aren't what you want them to be, you need to stop *allowing* that to continue. You've got to be the one to change it. Your mindset needs to change. It needs to accept more and expect abundance. I know it's a hard pill to swallow, but the reality is we get what we tolerate. Where you are now in life is the sum of the decisions you've made. The amount of money you earn, your career, your relationships—everything. If you don't *hate* your circumstances, you learn to *tolerate* them, therefore you make no changes because it doesn't bother you enough. There is a saying that "good is the enemy of great," and it is so true.

When you open your eyes in the morning, do you feel happiness? Do your feet hit the floor and you feel energized about attacking your day? Or do you hit snooze a few times, immediately think about what fires you must put out, and reluctantly get up? Do you determine what things you *must* do today to get you through to tomorrow? This is survival mode. Doing just enough to pay the bills and buy necessities and a few five-dollar coffees here and there. You stop aspiring for more on the premise that mediocre is somehow acceptable.

I'm not saying you shouldn't be grateful and humble. Certainly, there are people without their own homes to wake up in. For some, coffee isn't even a luxury they have access to. That's not what I'm saying here. I'm talking about ignoring your full capacity and settling for just enough. Getting by is not your purpose on this earth, and you know it. There are so many others in survival mode that it makes you feel like you're on the right path; there is a sense of belonging there. In fact, you'll convince yourself that you are doing okay compared to someone else who is struggling a little more than you are. In reality, though, you know you want more out of life.

Maybe you don't care if you have the most expensive car, but you want a nicer home for your family. A better school for your children. Maybe you'd like to help your mom or dad financially so they don't have to keep working so hard. Do you tolerate the education your children are receiving? Do you tolerate watching your mother or grandmother struggle? What are you tolerating right now? What have you been accepting, and is it time for you to recognize the things you *hate* and change them?

## BLISSFUL DISSATISFACTION

This term may seem to completely contradict itself, so let me explain. There are two sets of flawed thinking I see so many struggle with. The first is intentionally delaying happiness until a specific goal is achieved. "I'll be happy when—I have this house, this car, this relationship, etc." This delays a person's ability to be happy for a future destination and time. The problem with that thinking is that you still must bring *you* to that destination! If you have never learned to be happy where you are now, you are likely going to remain unhappy wherever you go, no matter what you achieve. It is possible to be happy on the journey to your goals. Learning to be happy in your current situation is a prerequisite to a fulfilling life.

The other flawed thinking is, "If I let myself enjoy this, I'll lose my drive." Many achievers think that if they allow themselves to be happy, it opens the door for potentially slowing down. Maybe even a total loss of ambition. What if they begin to settle for less than their goal? They believe that happiness will cause them to lose their edge. Nothing could be further from the truth.

People confuse happiness and satisfaction. They are totally different and independent states. You can be both blissful and dissatisfied simultaneously. In fact, the art of navigating these two states is a key to success and fulfillment.

Have you ever been really hungry and then bitten into a delicious meal, a meal that tasted so good that you literally feel blissful? When you felt that happiness, did the taste of that meal end your hunger? Did you feel like you wanted to stop right there? Or did it make you want even more? You weren't satisfied with just a taste—you were even hungrier for the next bite and wanted to finish it all! This is the same in every endeavor in life. Do not buy into the false belief that you need to delay your happiness until a future destination and time. Do not falsely believe you will lose your hunger if you allow joy, peace, and bliss into your life now!

The key to a fulfilling life is being happy while still desiring the next level. That is how to truly #MaxOut your life. Be blissfully dissatisfied.

## OVERNIGHT SUCCESS

Sustainable success is not built overnight. Real success is the result of consistent, sustained effort. Both wins and losses create the experience necessary to achieve success. Obstacles and rejections are strong components of the journey. I remember when I started my business there were days when I lost a potential client. I'd get in the car afterward and think, *"How can I do it better next time? How do I improve my responses to client questions? How could I have been better prepared?"*

Being rejected is an opportunity to grow and get better—period. Many times, it serves as a redirection for you, a necessary step to get you closer to your goals. In fitness, a muscle must be torn down to grow stronger. This is also true in life. The obstacles and rejections initially are painful, but when you look back on them, you realize they benefited you for the long-term goal. People respect experience, not shortcuts.

**Stop worrying!** Worry is wasted thought, energy, and emotion. It creates a worst-case scenario in your mind of an event that hasn't even happened yet and forces you to live through it! Most of the time, we will never even deal with the outcome we've worried ourselves sick over. Just stop! Worrying is pointless. There's no positive upside to it. The downside, however, comes with a stiff price. As we've learned, what we think about becomes our reality, so why on earth would we want to create a worse-case reality?

Always remember that champions take control of their lives, and they do this by controlling their thoughts and believing that the outcomes they desire *will* happen. They believe they are worthy of that outcome, and that belief creates their reality. You too can do the same thing.

**Worry does not take away tomorrow's troubles; it takes away today's peace.** Change what you think and believe, and you will transform your life.

**And lastly, a little about faith.** For me, personally, my faith is my foundation. My favorite scripture is Philippians 4:13: "I can do all things through

Christ who strengthens me." Every night I hit my knees and pray because I've had enough experiences in my life where my ego starts to get the advantage. Without a doubt, my hard work built the foundation of my success, but it's God's blessings that have allowed for it. The minute I start to forget that, the Lord has a way of reminding me. God's grace is such a beautiful thing.

If I look back at setbacks I've had in my life, they are typically the result of:

A.  I stopped doing the things I did to reach success.

B.  My ego started to take over, and that's when I must recommit to my faith.

I'm a big believer in planting the seeds and being consistent in planting those seeds across all areas of life—business, faith, fitness, relationships—and I know that if I keep doing what I need to do, God will take care of the harvest.

I have this overriding belief that if I keep doing things other people aren't willing to do, then I'm going to get things other people won't have.

Whatever your beliefs are, take time every day to practice them. Get strength, clarity, and grounding from them.

# 4

# #MAXOUT YOUR CONFIDENCE

*Changing Your Identity & Gaining Winning Confidence*

As I mentioned in my opening chapter, I struggled with my self-confidence. I mentioned the physical challenges I had as a child, but there were emotional challenges as well. I grew up in a great and loving family. A family that, like many, had some dysfunction from time to time. Our family has a history of having some dependency issues with drug and alcohol addiction. As a result, there was a dynamic in my household that, at times, cultivated uncertainty.

Between this dynamic and my physique, it isn't hard to understand why I started off withdrawn. All of these things contributed to my insecurities.

I've been able to overcome those insecurities using the techniques I am sharing with you here. Today, my confidence comes from the belief that I can do the necessary work to be great in my business, in my personal life, and with my fitness. I've built that reputation with myself over time, and that is what builds genuine confidence. Because I've consistently built the habit of keeping the promises I make to myself, I trust I can achieve the goals I set. I expect to achieve them. The very foundation of my confidence comes from this.

People who win are confident. People who struggle and lose lack confidence. If you don't *think* you're the best, how can you ever *become* the best? You've got to believe in yourself and that comes down to having confidence. Develop your confidence by keeping your promises to yourself.

## WHAT'S YOUR *IDENTITY?*

Our self-confidence, or what we believe we are worth, equals our *identity*. Our identity is how we see ourselves, and you can never (long-term) succeed beyond your identity.

The most powerful force in the human spirit is to live congruently with the ideas and beliefs that we hold true about ourselves. That self-image creates our identity. Identity is like a thermostat with a pre-set temperature.

*I want you to listen to me on this—this is the invisible force that dictates the entire direction of your life.*

You set the temperature for your life based on your identity.

The thermostat in a room that has been set to a specific temperature has the job of maintaining that specific temperature at all times. If a door is opened and a gust of cold air sweeps through the room, the thermostat kicks in and combats that cool air with heat to bring the temperature back to the pre-set degree. Same thing if the door is blown open with a gust of heat—the thermostat responds with cold air until the room is "back to normal." A good thermostat is never more than two degrees from its pre-set temperature.

*That pre-set temperature is your identity, and the thermostat (you) controls it.*

Think of it this way: If you have set that temperature at seventy-five degrees relating to money, happiness, success, fitness, love, etc., then no matter what happens in your life, that pre-set temperature will kick in.

If you heat up the conditions of your life to where things keep getting better and better, you will unconsciously turn on the AC to cool your success back down to that resting *identity belief* temperature of seventy-five degrees (self-sabotage). It will appear in ways that feel induced by circumstance and seem out of your control, but in reality, you've cooled your life back down to match your beliefs and identity.

The reverse is also true. If you start slipping too low, things start falling apart and you begin to really struggle, that heater of your life will kick in and warm things back up. You'll always find a way to get back on your feet and back to that seventy-five degrees.

It will always seem like you keep falling on hard times, or that you are just unlucky. Then suddenly, you'll get a little break, and things will go back to normal for a while. They may even get good again, and then sure enough, something will happen to bring you back down. Sound familiar?

Most people think the outside world will dictate your success. The truth is, it's an internal game, not external. You don't have control of outside elements (obstacles), but allowing them to impact your path to success *is* in your control. If you are in control of that thermostat (and you are), then regardless of the outside elements, you will find a way back to your identity temperature.

## SO, HOW DO WE RAISE OUR IDENTITY?

### 1. Through our associations.

If you are a "seventy-five degree identity", and you associate with people who are "one-hundred forty degree identity," you can't help but heat up your thermostat simply by being around them. When you are around successful people, you rise to meet that level of heat. Your associations are in your control. They are allowed into your room to heat it up versus allowing an external element (obstacles) in the door to cool you off. If you are not happy with a seventy-five-degree income or a seventy-five-degree education for your child, then you must get around people with the intensity and drive to heat you up.

Seek to add new associations in your circle to stretch your vision and give you reasons to raise your temperature. It has been said that you are the average of the five people closest to you. Do you know why? It's because proximity is power. We have multiple identities. Happiness, wealth, fitness, faith, etc. You may have a friend incredibly strong in faith, so they bring value in that area, but they are not in great shape, so they are not the same person you look to for guidance in fitness. If you notice you have no associations that challenge you or inspire you to improve to their level in an area of life, then it is crucial you change your associations immediately.

If your desire is to be wealthy, do you have wealthy friends? Or are all your friends broke and struggling? You can't be in a circle of successful, wealthy people if the only people you associate with are strugglers. The key to altering the direction of our life is to alter the temperature we are comfortable living in. That thermostat is the governor of your life, and until you can alter it, you will tolerate living at the temperature that is most comfortable. The next step will show you how to change that area.

## 2. Do a massive amount of work in a short amount of time.

Putting in a massive amount of work on a specific area alters our identity beliefs because we are doing things we've never done before. When you do this, you'll naturally start to believe that you're worth more because you are working harder.

If you normally make ten calls a day at the office, and now you're making one hundred, it won't be long until you believe that you are worthy of greater success because of it. If you're putting in more work, you will expect more gains.

**Nobody wins by working less.** Are you working hard? I mean *really* hard? Your #MaxOut level? The truth is, if you are not putting in the time, effort, and energy every single day, someone else is. Don't create an illusion of hard work—you can't cheat the grind. It knows.

## 3. Develop your confidence.

Self-confidence comes from keeping the promises you make to yourself. Self-confidence is, in truth, self-trust. You do this by building a relationship with yourself where you know *you* can trust *you*. As I mentioned earlier, self-confidence is the result of preparation and telling yourself you are going to do something and then doing it. It's simple. It's about creating trust and building a relationship with yourself, which changes your *identity belief* over time.

Confidence is not about being cocky. It's not arrogance, and it's not the opinion of others.

There is a reason I'm covering this again in depth. Self-confidence is also an internal game, not external. This is a huge discovery I've made in my life, and once I made it, it was liberating! I realized my self-confidence is in my control. *Self*-confidence is a reflection of how you feel about yourself, not how others perceive you. Having self-confidence (the way you treat yourself) serves as an instruction to others on how to treat you. I don't mean that you have the power to make people think a particular way about you. But your confidence informs others on what kind of attitude to have towards you (proactive). Letting others know how to *treat* you is more important than worrying about their *opinions* of you.

The truth is, people *aren't thinking about you* because they are thinking about what you think of them! Don't be dominated by people's thoughts, opinions, or judgments (reactive). Work hard for your own approval or God's approval—those are the only ones that matter.

Create a life that satisfies *you*.

If you are emotionally dependent on other people's approval, you will always be captive in a prison controlled by others. The irony is that these other people likely have very little long-term significance in your life, yet you're willing to give away your precious power, emotions, and control. The biggest dream killer of so many is their addiction to the opinions of others.

**Confident people take ownership of their faults and mistakes.** They are aware. They don't blame others for their failings or shortcomings. They have the confidence to admit when they are wrong and then the awareness to change it by moving forward. They are accountable.

**Get your uniform dirty.** All this thinking is great, but if you want to win, you've got to get out there and get dirty. When you take a chance and put your effort and work out into the world, it creates a wave of energy towards your goals, regardless of the result. It's a message to the world, to all those around you, and most importantly to yourself, that you are willing to accept the pain of loss as well as the reward of a win. People who are the most confident are the ones who've done the most work. Your work and effort strengthen you, positions you for wins, and prepares you for the life you are pursuing.

You cannot skip the work. Prepare yourself for the life you want. Put in the work so you are prepared to live the life you want.

# 5

# #MAXOUT YOUR BODY

## *Highest Possible Energy*

I believe it's of the utmost importance to take care of our physical body. It provides us the energy, confidence, and strength we need to win in business and in life. When we're fit, healthy, and active, we feel our best. Feeling good is important because our body is the temple of our soul and our mind, which is the source of our strength and power.

Keeping a healthy physical routine is one more way you are keeping a promise to yourself. It's a daily validation that you are worthy and value yourself enough to keep your promises to *you*.

Having a healthy, physical lifestyle gives you longevity and mental clarity, as well as building your self-confidence.

It's not about you looking like a bodybuilder or a supermodel. It's about keeping a daily routine that makes you feel your best, and it gives you the highest possible energy.

I'm so excited for you because, as you begin to transform your body, you will also be transforming your life! You've learned the skills to change your thinking, beliefs, and how to build strong supportive habits. Now you're taking all of that and applying it to getting in your best physical shape, which will reinforce your confidence, change your thinking, and overhaul your life. It is all tied together.

No matter where you are on your fitness journey, whether you are just starting out or are a seasoned pro, these tips can help you take it to the next level and get the results you want and deserve.

**My 10 tips for getting your body to its elite performance state.**

1. **Hire a trainer!** Go to the gym and hire someone to train you. They will teach you how to do the workouts to your best capability and how to do it correctly. They will also hold you accountable, which will help you make exercise a lifelong habit.

2. **Subscribe to fitness periodicals and social media** There are some great magazines such as *Men's Fitness*, *Muscle Magazine*, *Shape*, *Women's Fitness*, etc. that provide education, examples, and support. Additionally, a recent study showed the average person checks their smartphone eighty times a day. Following fitness influencers on social media and listening/watching podcasts are convenient ways to stay connected with your fitness mindset and goals.

3. **You cannot out-exercise a bad diet.** You must be focused on what you eat as much

or more than your physical training. It feeds your energy, performance, strength, and recovery. It's critical to getting the results you want.

4. **Drink lots of water.** It's 70% of your body so it should be 70% of what goes into your body. You need even more when you work out.

5. **Lighter weight is better** (assuming you aren't trying to build mass). Don't lift heavy weights when you're starting out— you're not impressing anyone! I'd rather have you lift lighter and do it correctly. This is important for beginners to prevent injury. Once you've mastered executing the exercises correctly, you can then add more weight.

6. **Morning.** I train in the morning because it gives me increased energy throughout my day. Everyone is different, but I noticed optimal results with morning workouts.

7. **Stretch.** I stretch fifteen minutes before and fifteen minutes after my daily workouts. This prevents injury, keeps you from getting sore, and increases flexibility.

8. **Music.** I always listen to music or inspirational podcasts to get to my peak performance state. You should consider listening to my #MaxOut podcast and other influencers during your workout. Making a strong playlist can help tap into your peak performance. Studies show that upbeat music can increase endurance by as much as 15%, and it serves as an excellent distraction from your side ache.

9. **5 and 5.** I work out five days a week and do five resistance exercises on each body part I'm targeting that day. Those of you just beginning need to start with a simple plan and routine that you adjust as you progress.

10. **Measure it.** Measure the amount of weight you use, the number of reps you can do,

record your weight/body fat, and track your progress. Without a point of measure, it is not possible to determine where you need to course correct. If it's been a while since you've stepped on the scale or faced your measurements, don't look at it negatively. Be excited to record them so you can compare your results. Everyone loves a good before and after picture. Be excited to create your own! Listen to more details at edmylett.com/podcasts "Ed's Fitness Regimen."

# 6

# #MAXOUT GOAL SETTING

## *Deadlines and Details*

**S**et goals as if you possess them. Be very specific with your goals. The three main elements necessary in achieving goals are *specificity*, *accountability*, and *visualization,*

Specificity is the first crucial step in goal setting. Your mind cannot go to work when this task is vague. Saying, "I want to be rich," is not a real goal. Identifying the amount of wealth you want, when you will achieve it, and what it will look like creates an actual target you can hit. The clearer it is, the more likely that your mind, body, and soul will go to work on creating those things in your life. The reason so many people do not achieve their goals is because they did not get specific and clear. People don't like being specific because it commits them to a target. They prefer to be vague so they can decide if they hit it or not.

The second essential step is *accountability*. There is power in saying the goal out loud and power in sharing it with someone that can hold you accountable. When life's distractions take you off track, having another person outside of those distractions can connect you back to those goals. Be accountable to a friend, family member, or mentor who can support you.

The third step is the *visualization* of your goals. This can be done by utilizing vision boards, posting your goal list throughout your home and office, or simply focusing on them in your mind repeatedly. If you are a praying person, you should pray about them. If you meditate, there are various types of meditation that allow you to focus on them. You should set time aside each day, at the same time of day, to visualize your goals. The more you focus on it, share it with others, and visualize it, the more familiar your brain becomes with it. The more familiar you are with your goals, the more likely you are to identify the paths, people, and tasks needed to achieve them. Obsessively create positive habits, and you can change and master any area of your life. Our minds love to gravitate towards the familiar.

Once you've set your goals and reasons, then you've got to write out a detailed plan of how to do it. Then review your goals, reasons, and plans every day. Your "why" is *seventy* times more powerful than your "how."

Do not undervalue the importance of writing out your plan and reasons. Structure serves as a map. If you're trying to navigate to a destination you've never been to, you will need a map to keep you on course. Your reasons (or your "whys") will fuel your perseverance when you come across obstacles along your journey.

If you have a goal to send your children to college, you should list a detailed savings plan that includes where to save, how much, and what you expect to have by a certain date. It should be accompanied with a picture of your child to give you a visual reminder of why you stay the course. When an obstacle such as an unexpected expense for your car or a break in your work decreases your income, you still find a way to fund that college dream for your child. You cut out expensive coffee, eating out, and other luxuries to ensure your goal is not sidelined for a temporary situation.

Goals are not promises; they are commitments. It's your *reasons,* not your *goals* that keep you from giving up. When something becomes important to you, your RAS will find it. Your mind will immediately go to work bringing you the resources and opportunities to help you achieve those goals. This is literally how and why your *obsessions become your possessions.*

**Make a real decision**. How do you know if you've made a real decision? If you followed it up with immediate action. The minute you decide something, *take quick action*. The only way to change your life is to make real decisions.

**Identify emotional reasons**. You must have an emotional attachment to your dreams. Build up the reasons that define why your goals matter. Your RAS can be supercharged with powerful reasons! Those reasons will elevate the price you are willing to pay and strengthen your will to win. I believe the stronger your will to win is, the less likely you are to sell it. There is no price you won't pay to achieve your goals. This is the part most people miss. You must have *emotional, compelling reasons* to keep you in the hunt for your dreams. Once you've made those reasons your passion, they become all the "inspiration" you need to fulfill your goals. For more details on goal setting, listen to the "Design Your Life" podcast at edmylett.com/podcasts.


**Touch your dreams.**

Give yourself the chance to experience some of the dreams you have. If there is a place you dream of living, you should visit the area and become familiar with it. Eat at the local restaurants or take your family to the park or beach near the homes you dream of living in. Or maybe you have a car you dream of owning. You should test drive it so your mind becomes familiar with it. Take a mini-vacation for a couple days with your family someplace beautiful and a bit out of reach for you financially. I'm not saying to spend money you don't have to pretend you are somewhere you are not; I'm suggesting you allow yourself to experience the type of lifestyle you dream of so you can become familiar with it. The more familiar your brain becomes with your dreams, the more you believe you belong in them. Again, your thoughts are primarily the same ones over and over. You need to replace old ones that don't serve you with the ones you want to become your reality. Go touch your dreams.

# 7

# #MAXOUT YOUR WILL TO WIN

*Can You Be Bought?*

Can you be bought? Is your will to win for sale?

Most people allow their will to win to have a price. Their dreams have a price. Their children's dreams have a price. With enough rejection, enough pain and setbacks, most people will relent, selling their will to win. By doing this, they are selling out not just their dreams but their destiny and their family. They will sell out because the price got too high.

People who are winners negotiate their price in advance. They know what their dreams and their destiny are worth long before it ever gets tested. Those that have not yet committed don't know what that price is. That is why it's so easy for obstacles to persuade them to give up and sell out. They will call it something else. They'll say, "Oh, it wasn't for me." "The timing wasn't right." "I didn't have a mentor and didn't know what I was doing." They'll have plenty of excuses as to why they sold their dreams, but the truth is that they sold out. They couldn't handle the heat. The price got too high and they weren't ready to pay it. That's the truth.

When I was broke and coming from a place of scarcity, I would walk into a store and ask, "How much does it cost?" I would look at the price tag first. It's the same way in life. When you are approaching your life and your dreams from a place of scarcity, you are always asking yourself, "What's the price?" You are always weighing if the risk and work are worth the reward. When you do that, it's constantly draining your focus because you're always renegotiating the price. When resources are limited, the focus is placed on price (cost) to see what is affordable. I want you to focus on *worth,* not cost.

If you were shopping for a birthday gift, you likely have an idea of what your max dollar amount to spend is. And if you think about it, you'll base it on who you are buying the gift for. (We're going to get very honest here). Let's just say you are looking at a beautiful scarf as the gift. If you are buying it for a colleague at the office, you flip over the tag to evaluate if that cost is in line with what you were willing to spend. If it's too high, you will quickly move on to find something in the range you've allotted.

Now, if the gift is for your sick mother and you are not sure exactly how many more birthdays she will have, you don't flip that tag to inspect the cost. You just buy it because you know her happiness is *worth* whatever the cost of that scarf.

If your income level is too low to provide the quality of life you want for yourself and your family, what have you done to change that? Could you fight for a promotion? Start a side business? Learn a new skill set to increase your ability to earn a higher income? It's absolutely 100% in your control, so why do you stay in the same spot?

Most people are not willing to put in the extra work to better themselves. They fall into the pattern of working a job they don't like for just enough money to pay for a handful of bills and a modest lifestyle. *A wage is nothing more than a bribe a business owner has paid someone to work on his or her dreams instead of their own.*

Instead of going for what they want, they allow their scarcity mentality to dictate what they can have. Life should be about chasing what you really want, not accepting what is left over. If you obsess over the cost of your dreams, you will *never* pay the price for them; you will just keep re-negotiating them.

Higher, elevated thinking is focusing on worth, not cost. What is your child's future worth? What is the security of your family worth to you? Your own happiness and quality of life—what is it *worth*? There are no numbers imaginable to answer these questions. The answer is that they are valuable beyond measure. Yet, you continue to flip over the tags of life and assess their cost.

If you have *truly* committed to your dreams, there is no obstacle (price tag) too big. You will find a way to overcome it because from the start you already decided the worth of your dreams. Nothing can make you quit. Your will to win is not for sale.

Conversely, your will to win must be guarded against success. As you progress and achieve milestones, do not allow that progress to cloud the vision to your ultimate goal. Small wins create the illusion that you are successful, and you start to take your foot off the gas. You stop investing the effort that caused you to succeed, and eventually, you begin to regress. Once you sense this, you may start to alter the goal. You'll tell yourself, "This is good enough," and convince yourself that you never really wanted the initial goal. You settle for less than your dreams. This is why your identity is so important. If your result exceeds your thermostat, you will cool life down and rationalize your way back to your true identity.

Don't settle for *just enough* money, accolades, and short-term success. Don't stop working hard and doing the things that brought you success. The real achievers develop themselves and discover innovative ways to elevate their strategies.

From the beginning, make the decision to not be bought with failure *or* success. Set your goals so that you know what the ultimate version of your dream looks like, and then let *nothing* distract you from achieving it.

For more details on how to figure out your recipe for winning, listen to my podcast on iTunes or go to edmylett.com/podcasts and listen to "Unlocking Your Success Code."

# FINAL THOUGHTS

My intent with this book was to share the steps I took to produce results in my own life. I broke them down into the main subjects of habits, mind, confidence, fitness, goal setting, and will. There is still much more to explore on our roads to success, but the details here should serve as a strong start. I have a few more thoughts to share that I feel are important.

**Chasing Butterflies.** We've all had that butterfly feeling before. You know that feeling I'm talking about? That tickle in your stomach? Maybe as you stepped on the field of a big game in high school, when you sat in the waiting room for an important interview or when you walked down the aisle of your wedding. The uncertainty of conquering your biggest dreams will give you butterflies. When is the last time you got those butterflies? If you're not experiencing butterflies as you work towards your dreams, then you're not chasing your true destiny. The quality of your life is in direct proportion to the amount of times you get to experience the feelings of uncertainty. When we are young, we actually chased those butterflies. As we get older, we tend to avoid the feeling of uncertainty. All the greatest memories in your life happened right after the butterflies. In fact, God gives us those butterflies to let us know we are on track to our dreams and our destiny. Butterflies are memory makers. The key to a rich and fulfilled existence is a #MaxOut life full of those butterfly moments. I have a feeling when I meet that ultimate version of me; all we are going to discuss are *butterfly moments.*

Put yourself in situations where you'll be uncertain. Don't be afraid to get uncomfortable.

The feeling of being *alive* often comes with the feeling of uncertainty. It's what makes you step up your game and truly experience life to the fullest. When you begin to take your life in a new direction, some people are not going to support or believe in you. If you're addicted to what other people think, you're going to fail quickly. There are going to be haters, and people will be jealous of you. Deciding to change your life—whether it be your body, relationships, or finances— means you need to accept from the very beginning that not everybody will be on board.

All millionaires and billionaires were once laughed at. I was laughed at and rejected. I had family members ridicule me. I had people try to talk me out of my business and tell me to get a real job. It's the price you pay for chasing greatness. Anyone chasing a big dream will face ridicule and rejection. Even when you win, people will talk bad about you. Get over it.

**There are three things** that contribute to the caliber of your life and the emotions associated with it:

1. The caliber of your relationships

2. The caliber of your beliefs

3. The caliber of the questions you ask yourself (i.e. your thinking)

**Your life is like a movie.** Most of our beliefs are acquired during our childhood when we're young and defenseless. Our parents and their beliefs primarily influenced our beliefs and shaped our adult mindset. If we are not aware of the beliefs that don't serve us, they begin to take control of our life's script.

How many people do you know who are in the career their parents wanted them to be in? Or people who are doing what everyone expected them to do? Or what society told them to do?

Most people go through life with a script some-one else has written for them. You can change the story and script at any point. Change it now! In your life, as with any good script, the main characters matter the most. The main characters are you and a few core supporting cast members, not the extras! Not the background people.

Have you ever watched the end of the movie and watched the credits? After all the leading characters are listed, there becomes a laundry list of extras that really aren't integral to the story; they are extras. Cab driver #2, bouncer #1—they don't even have names. No one even remembers them, yet most people allow the "extras" to dominate the script of their lives. We care too much of what the extras think about us.

When you realize that you are the lead character in the story of your life, you unleash a force within you that is incredibly powerful. You and God get to write your own script. Once you take control of that script and step into your own leading role, the one you've written for yourself, your subconscious mind will go to work on attracting the perfect supporting cast and attracting the perfect set.

Think of who is in your main cast. Picture their faces right now. Are they your kids? Your spouse? Your parents? There's only about half a dozen of these people in our life, the ones who really matter. What will they say about you when your story is over?

You decide. You are writing the script.

Don't be surprised if some of your main cast members question your decisions and push back on your dreams. You will be challenged to defend your choices and stand your ground. This will not always be easy, but it will strengthen the roots to your dreams.

Other people don't control you or your life, nor do they control your beliefs or emotions. Learned helplessness is the crippling mindset that other people are the ones doing things *to you*. But the reality is that everything in your life is happening for you, not to you. All the experiences, trials, obstacles, and struggles you've gone through have happened *for* you.

I mentioned in my first chapter how, in hindsight, the end of my baseball career was a blessing in disguise. If that didn't happen, my life would have gone in a completely different direction. Hindsight is the understanding of a situation or event only after it has happened. One of the traits I've developed over the years is the ability to have that same hindsight clarity while in the present. In other words, I have developed the ability to see the benefit of an obstacle while going through the adversity. The normal reaction of adversity is to be frustrated and allow it to slow your progress, or worse, create doubt. If you can learn to see the benefit of the adversity at the time it is happening, you will start to separate your level of thinking from average to elite.

**You get what you expect**. At the end of the day, you get your standards. Raise your expectations of yourself and hold yourself to the highest standards. Setting the bar high for yourself keeps you sharp, leaves an elevated impression on others, and develops your confidence. Average people tend to look for shortcuts and give minimum effort. When you maintain those high standards, you separate yourself from average. Don't let the average set a ceiling on your capacity. Don't let the fears of others be your fears. Don't let the lower expectations of others set the bar for what is possible for you.

Make decisions, set standards, and take actions that will get you closer to becoming the best version of you and the person you were born to be. You have it within you. I'm no different than you. I wasn't born with a magic gene that you don't have; I just wanted to win so bad that I didn't allow anyone or anything to steal my dreams.

Procrastination is a thief, and fear is a liar. You were destined for a life of abundance and prosperity. Your maker didn't put you here to just get by. You put in the work, so you expect to win! Never again allow fear to paralyze you. You've made *no* decisions until action is taken.

As I said in the beginning of this book, I'm chasing down the ultimate version of me. The day will come when I get to be face-to-face with the destiny version of me. I want the satisfaction of knowing I spent a lifetime chasing down this man, and that in the end, I caught up with him. That he and I are identical. That I challenged myself, I took risks, I dug deeper, I put in the work, and I gave it all I had. I used every ounce of blessing God gave me and left nothing in the tank. It's the driving force in my life.

I want you to push yourself now more than you ever have in your life. You have so much more in you. You have gifts and talents that you've likely not tapped into because you just didn't know how. Maybe you just need a different environment to utilize them or a mentor to help you discover them. Maybe you just need someone to believe in you. Well, I believe in you, and that makes two, so let's go!

Take immediate, massive action and go win! It's my prayer that you feel a call to change in your soul and come out swinging. That you picture your life and the lives of your family living their true destiny. Now is the time to become the person you were destined to be. The ultimate #MaxOut version of you.

*Join the conversation! I'd love to connect with you. Share your thoughts and comments about what you've learned with me on social media. Be sure to follow on Instagram @EdMylett, Twitter @EdMylett, and Facebook. And don't forget you can always continue to learn by listening to my weekly podcast on iTunes: Max Out with Ed Mylett, on my YouTube channel: Ed Mylett, or by visiting my website at edmylett.com.*